Fingerpicking
Gershwin

by John Miller

© 1980 Amsco Music Publishing Company
A Division of Music Sales Corporation, New York
All Rights Reserved

International Standard Book Number: 0-8256-2215-8

Distributed throughout the world by Music Sales Corporation:

33 West 60th Street, New York 10023
78 Newman Street, London W1P 3LA
27 Clarendon Street, Artarmon, Sydney NSW 2064
Kölner Strasse 199, D-5000, Cologne 90

To my parents, Clarence and Hope Miller

Cover design by David M. Nehila
Book design by Katrina Orlowsky
Edited by Peter Pickow

Acknowledgements

My deepest thanks
to George Gershwin, for the wonderful songs, which remain as marvelous
gifts to all of us.

Thanks as well to
Jason Shulman, for giving me the opportunity to write this book.
Peter Pickow, for his valuable editorial assistance and advice.
Everyone else who helped make this book a reality.

Preface

The music of George Gershwin defies easy categorization. It is equally at home in cabaret or concert hall and is as fresh and exciting today as it was when it was composed more than forty years ago. In some undefinable way, Gershwin's music has a special meaning for lovers of American music.

The guitar is a great medium for George Gershwin's music. The rich harmonies and unforgettable melodies transfer gracefully to the guitar, and the fingerpicking guitarist is able to bring out the rhythmic subtleties so characteristic of Gershwin's music. In arranging these fifteen songs, I have taken care to preserve those harmonies, melodies, and rhythms. At the same time, I have tried to take advantage of the peculiar musical possibilities which the guitar presents to a musician: the opportunities to play drones, slides, unisons, and all the other effects so near and dear to every guitarist's heart. Otherwise, you may as well play the songs on a calliope!

Good luck and have fun!

Contents

Introduction

Two notational systems have been employed in this book: standard musical notation and tablature (TAB). In the standard notation, all the music appears on a treble staff, the direction of each note's stem indicating whether it is picked by the thumb or fingers of the right hand. Key signatures and rhythmic values are designated in the usual fashion. The TAB is also of the standard variety, although it is made perhaps a bit more complicated than usual by the introduction of a few new techniques and their symbols into the terminology. For those of you who are unfamiliar with tablature, it is a musical shorthand indicating left-hand position through the use of fret numbers diagrammed on the six strings of the guitar. Rhythmic notation is the same in TAB as in standard notation, and just as in standard notation, the stem direction of a note indicates whether it is picked by the thumb or fingers. A few basic chord positions are included after each song.

Regarding the relative merits of standard notation versus TAB, I'd say that each has its strengths and weaknesses. Standard notation is good because it makes pitch values and melody clear to the player in a way that TAB, with its fret-number indications can not. TAB, however, is much more explicit than standard notation with regard to the actual execution, and has the extra advantage of clarifying the exact position on the neck for each note. Between the two systems, you should be able to get a pretty clear picture of how an arrangement should sound and how to go about playing it.

The use of a capo is suggested for most of the songs in this book. In the songs where a capo is suggested, standard notation and TAB will always be relative to capo placement. In other words, an arrangement that is played out of a D major will always be notated in the key of D, whether capo placement is called for on the first, second, or third fret (or wherever). This allows those of you who, for religious or legal reasons are unable to use a capo, to play these arrangements without having to perform the thankless task of transposition.

One further note regarding rhythmic notation in these arrangements: I have tried to be scrupulous about rhythmic and durational values, to the extent that the thumb and fingers of the right hand have separate rests indicated. In addition, rhythmic values show how long a particular chordal position or note is actually held. Thus, the rhythmic notation ends up showing not only the usual features such as time signature, pulse, syncopations, *et al;* but also indicates left-hand movement. I guess it's my own pet peeve, but I've often felt that rhythm was treated like a poor relation compared to harmony and melody in most notational systems. It was not for nothing that Duke Ellington observed, "It Don't Mean a Thing if It Ain't Got That Swing." As much as possible, I've tried to write the swing *into* these arrangements.

Enough explanation, now for terms:

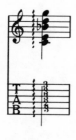

a thumb glissando or strum. All notes should be strummed by the thumb of the right hand.

A finger strum. All notes should be lightly brushed by the fingers of the right hand in the direction of *treble to bass.*

ditto last definition, but direction of the strum is reversed.

a technique in which the right hand is dropped on the strings. The heel of the hand damps the strings while the little finger lightly taps the top of the guitar. This is strictly a rhythmic effect.

This symbol is used to indicate an unaccented or squelched note. This effect may be achieved either by lack of emphasis in the right-hand touch, or by left-hand damping; i.e., only partially depressing the string at the fret indicated.

slide: Only the first note is picked by the right hand. The second is produced by sliding the fretting finger to it while still depressing the string.

pull-off: Once again, only the first note is picked by the right hand. The second is produced by the fretting finger pulling off the string so that the second note, fretted or not, is made clearly audible.

hammer-on: Roughly opposite to the pull-off. The first note is picked by the right hand and the second is produced by fretting the given string as indicated.

stretch or bend: Unless otherwise indicated, the note in question is stretched about ½ step.

Well, I guess that about covers it. Now you just have to step it up and go!

Love Is Here to Stay

"Our Love Is Here to Stay" is a graceful ballad from the show *An American in Paris*. This arrangement makes frequent use of the thumb glissando, a right-hand technique which will often be employed throughout the book. The thumb gliss, which is really no more than a strum, may be executed as follows: Curve the thumb of the right hand back on itself in a crescent shape and strum the designated strings with the tip of the thumb next to the nail *in one motion*. Do not pick each string separately. The thumb gliss should produce a silvery ringing sound. Remember to keep an eye (ear?) on those quarter-note triplets.

capo third fret
(key of F) ♩=108

George and Ira Gershwin

7

Bidin' My Time

Don't let the $\frac{12}{8}$ time signature scare you. It's just a translation into notation of what is usually referred to as "Swing." The new right-hand technique here is the finger-strum and simultaneous damp; for example,

As the TAB indicates ↓ , give the designated strings a light upward brush, picking up the right hand as you do so. With ↑ , drop the right hand back down, brushing the designated strings at the same time. If the symbol ↑ is accompanied by the asterisk, ↑ , damp the strings with the heel of the right hand and lightly tap the top of the guitar with your little finger as you brush the strings. Sometimes the damp and tap, * , appears without the strum.

Fortunately, these techniques are harder to explain than they are to do! When you get the strums and damps going smoothly, the effect is as though you had a drummer accompanying you on a high-hat. Surely this is a desirable aural sensation.

capo third fret (key of E♭) ♩=114

George and Ira Gershwin

Fascinating Rhythm

This version of "Fascinating Rhythm" is especially designed for all you fans of contrapuntal arrangements out there. No verse, just chorus here. Playing the melody in eighth notes rather than broken triplets gives the rhythm a funny, jerky, Chaplinesque feel. When the song comes out of the contrapuntal section in measure nine, the melody should really sing out. I play the ascending bass run in measure fifteen by changing directions with my thumb, but you may find some other method more comfortable.

capo first fret
(key of Bb) ♩=140

George and Ira Gershwin

14

Liza

"Liza" has a charming, slightly archaic quality that makes it reminiscent of the pop music of the 1890s; it's really a cakewalk. The gradually ascending progression of the chorus has made it a great favorite of jazz players and terrific versions (which could hardly be more different from each other) have been recorded by Benny Goodman, Django Reinhardt and Stephane Grappelli, and Thelonious Monk. No new techniques here, just make sure you get that light, swinging feel.

capo first fret
(key of B♭) ♩=116

George Gershwin and Gus Kahn

But Not for Me

"But Not for Me" is one of Gershwin's most beautiful ballads. Once again, there is extensive use of thumb glisses. Don't feel compelled to play this arrangement in strict mentronomic time. "But Not for Me" cries out for a rhythmically expansive treatment with lots of rubato. Strive for a dramatically different expression in each section. This arrangement may be heard on *Safe Sweet Home* (Rounder Records 3016).

23

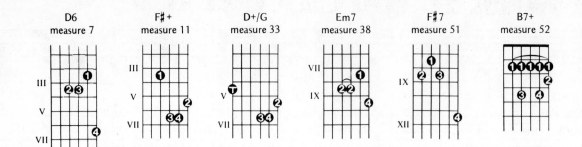

Nice Work if You Can Get It

In this tune, George Gershwin gives us another of the imaginative treatments of a circle-of-fifths progression that we have come to expect of him. It has the swinging rhythm so characteristic of many of his songs. There are some rather quick shifts in left-hand position here. Make sure (in general) that you aren't holding the neck of the guitar as though it were a baseball bat. In order to achieve maximum left-hand agility and quickness, the crotch formed by the thumb and index finger of the left hand should not touch the neck of the guitar. Freeing the left hand in this way should also help you get clean-sounding barres and reach some of those stretches you may encounter from time to time in these arrangements.

26

Oh, Lady Be Good!

Sometimes the treatment of a song by a great musician will forever after affect our perspective. Take "Lady Be Good," for instance. The original tempo marking is *Allegretto grazioso*, but after hearing Ella Fitzgerald's astonishing rendition, I have never been able to think of "Lady Be Good" as anything but a very up-tempo rhythm song. This version reflects Miss Fitzgerald's influence. The verse should be played in a "comic-spooky" manner and the chorus "as a bat out of Hell." As a bonus, this has probably the least difficult left-hand part of any song in the book.

capo third fret
(keys of Am and C) ♩.=110

George and Ira Gershwin

Chorus (♩.=176)

Embraceable You

"Embraceable You" is one of Gershwin's best-loved songs. The parenthetical fingering in the left-hand diagram for measure twenty-one is intended to designate a note which is not plucked by the right hand, but hammered by the left. The same method will be used to diagram notes which are pulled off or slid into, later in the book. The melody in the opening of the chorus (measures twenty-one, twenty-two, thirty-seven, and thirty-eight) is voiced so that the thumb picks it. You should strive for a round, penetrating tone here. The rhythm should be free, with lots of rubato.

capo first fret
(key of D♭) ♩=106

George and Ira Gershwin

Chorus

Of Thee I Sing

"Of Thee I Sing" is somewhat of an anomaly; it's a wistful march. This arrangement introduces the infamous practice of capo-sliding in measure eight. To execute this, pick the C♯7 chord and (while still holding the chord) reach up with the right hand to pull the capo up the neck two frets. This will require a lot of practice before you're able to do it smoothly without breaking the rhythmic flow. In fact I know of only one kind of capo that will permit this technique: The Bill Russell Elastic Capo. Remember: All notation is relative to capo placement, so the frame of reference changes from the first to the third fret as the capo slides.

38

Blah, Blah, Blah

"Blah, Blah, Blah" is one of George Gershwin's prettiest and yet least well-known songs. Gershwin was fond of a sort of locked parallel chord-movement which I have kept intact in this arrangement (see measures twenty-nine, thirty, thirty-three, and forty-five). Be sure to observe all fingerings as designated in the diagrams and to hit the strings firmly enough so that all hammer-ons and slides are audible, clear, and bright.

capo third fret
(keys of F and B♭) ♩=118

George and Ira Gershwin

42

I Got Rhythm

For at least thirty years, "I Got Rhythm" was *the* tune on which jazz improvisers cut their teeth and did their hottest playing. This version is designed to convince any skeptics out there that the title's claim is gospel truth. The seldom-used closed-B♭ position gives this arrangement a dense, chunky sound. On the bridge (measures seventeen through twenty-three) the left hand is bounced, fully depressing the strings on the first and third beats, and only partially depressing the strings on the second and fourth beats. This left-hand bouncing results in the damping represented in the TAB by the symbol ⌒. Between ⌒ and ＊, there's a whole lot of damping going on!

George and Ira Gershwin

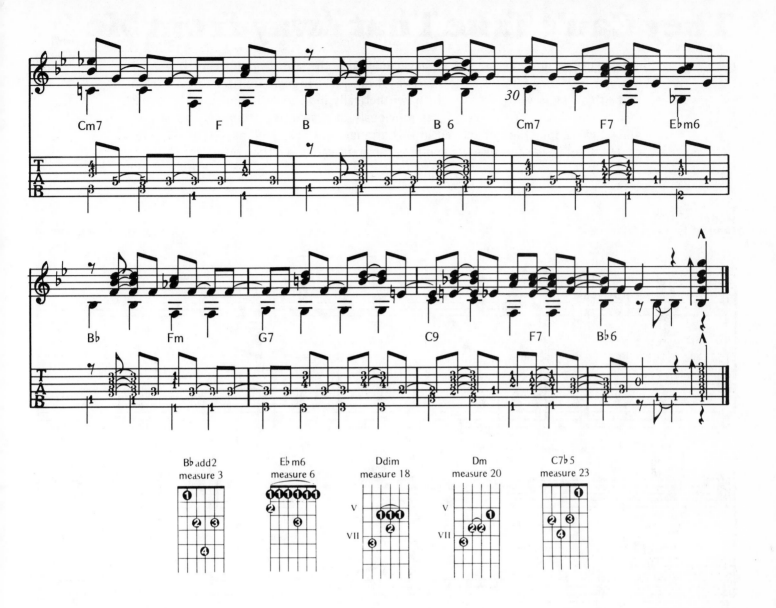

They Can't Take That Away from Me

It's hard to imagine any other singer matching the style and grace Fred Astaire brought to "They Can't Take That Away from Me." In measure fifty-three, stretch that 6th string, seventh fret, to the parenthetically indicated pitch of the 5th string, second fret. Many of the techniques previously discussed (e.g. thumb glisses, strumming and damping) are employed in this arrangement. Try and make those sexy repeated notes in the chorus say something different each time they return.

50

The Man I Love

"The Man I Love" is one of George Gershwin's most dramatic songs. Interestingly enough, it was not an immediate hit and took some time to achieve block-buster status. The most difficult parts of this version are the sixteenth-note slides in measures twenty-five through twenty-nine. After a great deal of experimentation, I found that the following technique yielded the best results on the slides: All slides should be played with the third finger of the left hand. Rather than attempting to move the third finger alone, fix its position relative to the hand and move the entire hand down the neck. This should enable you to achieve a clear, rhythmically even slide. The bridge of the chorus (measures thirty-three through forty) should feature a marked accelerando. This song is more effective when played slowly, but try to avoid an extreme dirge-like tempo.

capo first fret
(key of E♭) ♩=104

George and Ira Gershwin

Someone to Watch over Me

"Someone to Watch over Me" is the first Gershwin song I ever transcribed and it is still one of my favorites. Change your tone and volume to delineate the different sections of the song. This version is available on *How About Me?* (Blue Goose Records 1012).

George and Ira Gershwin

57

58

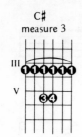

C#
measure 3

B6
measure 6

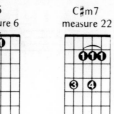

C#m7
measure 22

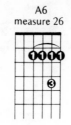

A6
measure 26

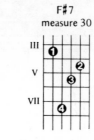

F#7
measure 30

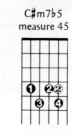

C#m7♭5
measure 45

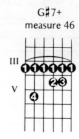

G#7+
measure 46

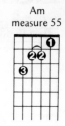

Am
measure 55

Love Walked In

I guess it's my prerogative to save the best for last; "Love Walked In" is my favorite George Gershwin song. Flawless conception and a beautiful, singing line are the hallmarks of this lovely song. No new techniques here, just the elusive goal of playing this song as well as it was written.

capo first fret
(key of E♭) ♩=110

George and Ira Gershwin

Chorus

62

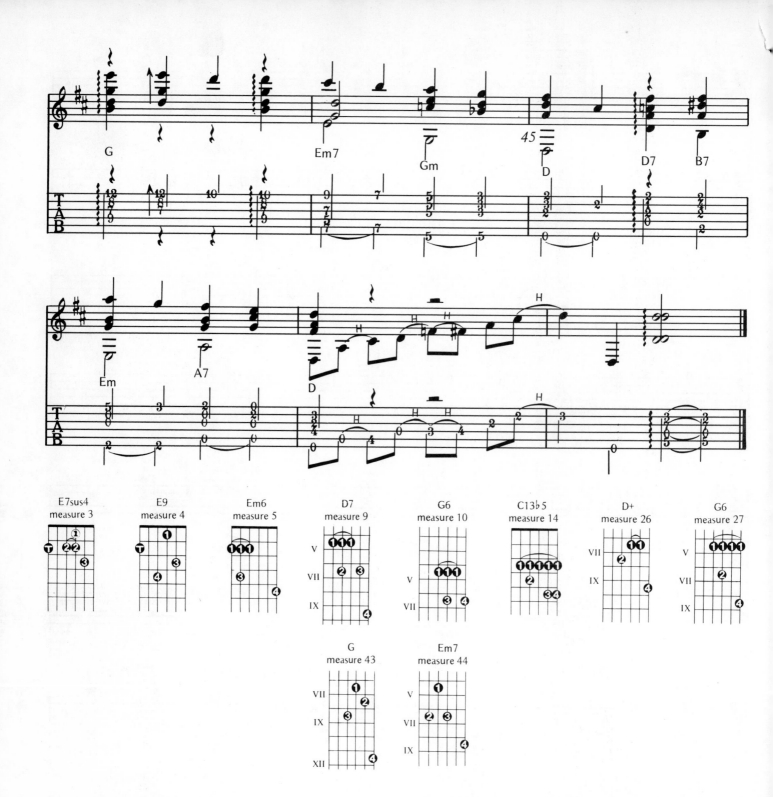